Is It Wrong to
EAT MEAT?

By Kate Rogers

Published in 2019 by
KidHaven Publishing, an Imprint of Greenhaven Publishing, LLC
353 3rd Avenue
Suite 255
New York, NY 10010

Designer: Deanna Paternostro
Editor: Katie Kawa

Photo credits: Cover Happy cake Happy cafe/Shutterstock.com; pp. 5 (top), 9 a katz/ Shutterstock.com; p. 5 (bottom) BlueOrange Studio/Shutterstock.com; pp. 7, 21 (inset, middle-left) Alexander Prokopenko/Shutterstock.com; p. 11 (top) alexkich/Shutterstock.com; p. 11 (bottom) GUDKOV ANDREY/Shutterstock.com; p. 13 acceptphoto/Shutterstock.com; p. 15 Monkey Business Images/Shutterstock.com; p. 17 108MotionBG/Shutterstock.com; p. 19 Aksinia Abiagam/ Shutterstock.com; p. 21 (notepad) ESB Professional/Shutterstock.com; p. 21 (markers) Kucher Serhii/ Shutterstock.com; p. 21 (photo frame) FARBAI/iStock/Thinkstock; p. 21 (inset, left) Phil's Mommy/ Shutterstock.com; p. 21 (inset, middle-right) 1968/Shutterstock.com; p. 21 (inset, right) behzad moloud/Shutterstock.com.

Cataloging-in-Publication Data

Names: Rogers, Kate.
Title: Is it wrong to eat meat? / Kate Rogers.
Description: New York : KidHaven Publishing, 2019. | Series: Points of view | Includes glossary and index.
Identifiers: ISBN 9781534525764 (pbk.) | 9781534525757 (library bound) | ISBN 9781534525771 (6 pack) | ISBN 9781534525788 (ebook)
Subjects: LCSH: Meat–Moral and ethical aspects–Juvenile literature. | Animal welfare–Juvenile literature. | Vegetarianism–Juvenile literature.
Classification: LCC TX373.R64 2019 | DDC 338.1'76–dc23

Printed in the United States of America

CPSIA compliance information: Batch #BS18KL: For further information contact Greenhaven Publishing LLC, New York, New York at 1-844-317-7404.

Please visit our website, www.greenhavenpublishing.com. For a free color catalog of all our high-quality books, call toll free 1-844-317-7404 or fax 1-844-317-7405.

CONTENTS

To Eat or Not
TO EAT?

Some people love to eat meat. They enjoy chicken, steak, hamburgers, and other food that was once a live animal. Other people, however, choose not to eat meat. They do this for different reasons, including a belief that this will make them healthier.

Another reason people don't eat meat is because they believe it's wrong to kill and eat animals. Their point of view **affects** what they choose to eat. People who eat meat generally have an opposing point of view. They don't believe they're doing anything wrong when they eat meat. Read on to learn more about both sides of this **debate**!

Know the Facts!

One of the most famous groups that speaks out against eating meat is People for the Ethical Treatment of Animals (PETA).

Do you believe it's wrong to eat meat? Before you answer that question, it's important to find out facts you can use to support your opinion.

Vegetarians and
VEGANS

A vegetarian is a person who doesn't eat meat. This generally also includes fish, other sea animals such as shrimp or clams, and poultry, which are birds such as chickens that are raised to feed people. Some vegetarians eat other foods that come from animals. These include dairy products, such as milk and cheese, and eggs.

Other people don't eat or use anything that comes from animals. This includes meat, dairy products, eggs, and even honey because it comes from bees. People who follow this way of living are known as vegans.

Know the Facts!

A 2016 study showed that 9 percent of adults in the United States said they're vegetarian or vegan.

Vegans believe people don't have a right to use animals for anything, including food. These are some of the foods vegans don't eat because they believe it's wrong.

Animal RIGHTS

Many people become vegetarians or vegans because they support the animal rights movement. This movement was founded on the belief that animals should be valued for more than what they can give to people.

People who feel this way about animals believe it's wrong to kill a creature just so we can eat it. They also think it's wrong to make animals suffer because animals can feel pain. Many people who choose not to eat meat believe their choice will save some animals' lives.

Know the Facts!

Animal Liberation, which was written by Peter Singer and **published** in 1975, is often called the most important book in the animal rights movement. Many of the beliefs of vegans and vegetarians come from this book.

Some people feel very strongly about animal rights. They believe eating meat is cruel, or unkind.

People as
PREDATORS

People who eat meat often don't think about animal rights. In some cases, they don't believe animals have rights, so they're not bothered by eating animals. They believe eating meat isn't wrong because animals can't think the way people can.

They also argue that people aren't the only living things that eat meat. Other animals do it, too. Some animals are predators, and some animals are prey that are hunted and eaten by predators. Using this way of thinking, people claim that humans are no different from other predators, such as lions or bears.

Know the Facts!

An animal that only eats meat is known as a carnivore. Most people are omnivores, or creatures that eat both meat and plants.

Some people believe humans who hunt and eat animals
aren't different from other natural predators,
so they shouldn't have to feel bad about eating meat.

Factory
FARMING

One of the main reasons people feel it's wrong to eat meat is the way animals are often treated before becoming food for people. Many animals are raised in factory farms, which are large, indoor farms. Factory farms are often crowded, and the animals aren't generally taken outside. They live in cages or pens for their whole life.

Animals in factory farms are often fed things they're not meant to eat. For example, cows are sometimes fed corn when their bodies are built to eat grass. This isn't healthy for animals.

Know the Facts!

Factory farming produces 99 percent of the meat eaten in the United States.

Factory farming is practiced in the United States and around the world because it's a cheap way to raise many animals in one place.

Other
CHOICES

Many people who eat meat also believe that factory farming is cruel. Instead of choosing to eat all meat, they choose to only eat meat that comes from places other than factory farms. Although factory farming produces most of the meat people eat, it's not the only way to raise animals for food.

Some people choose to eat free-range meat, such as chicken. Free-range chickens are allowed to go outside, unlike chickens raised in factory farms. This makes people feel better about eating meat because the animals lived a better, healthier life before becoming food.

Know the Facts!

The U.S. Department of Agriculture (USDA) is the part of the U.S. government in charge of farming.

14

People can read the labels on the meat they buy to learn how the animal they're eating was raised. This can help people make choices to only eat meat from farms that treat their animals well.

Harming the
ENVIRONMENT

People around the world are working to keep the earth safe and clean. Some of them believe not eating meat is a way to do this. They think it's wrong to eat meat because raising animals for food is bad for the **environment**.

Factory farms create pollution, which harms the earth. Raising animals for food also requires a large amount of fresh water and land, which are already in short supply. Trees, which are needed for clean air, are sometimes cut down to make room for farms and **ranches**.

Know the Facts!

According to a 2009 study, more than 80 percent of the deforestation, or cutting down of trees, in the **Amazon rain forest**, was done to create cattle ranches.

Some people believe it's wrong to eat meat because animals raised for food are given grain that could be used to keep millions of people from going hungry.

Meat on the
BRAIN

Some people argue that if it's wrong to eat meat, our bodies wouldn't be built to do it. Humans have eaten meat for millions of years, and some scientists believe eating meat helped the human brain become more advanced. Eating meat allowed early humans to take in more calories than they could by eating only plants. This allowed their brains to grow.

Also, animal products, such as meat and eggs, are the only natural way to get **vitamin** B12. The human body needs this vitamin for many tasks, including making red blood cells.

Know the Facts!

Meat became a major part of the human **diet** around 2.6 million years ago.

The human body's need for vitamin B12 is sometimes used as **proof** that people are supposed to eat animal products.

Respecting Other Points of
VIEW

People make many choices every day about the food they eat. In some cases, they make the choice not to eat meat because they believe eating meat is unhealthy or wrong. In other cases, they choose to eat meat because they like how it tastes and don't believe there's anything wrong with it.

Not everyone makes the same choices about food, and people sometimes judge others based on the food they choose to eat or not to eat. However, it's important to understand why people make the choices they do. This can help you treat everyone with respect.

Know the Facts!

Meatless Monday is an initiative, or plan, that started in 2003 to encourage people to stop eating meat on Mondays.

Is it wrong to eat meat?

YES

- Animals have rights, which are taken away when they're killed for food.

- Animals can feel pain, so killing them for food is cruel.

- Factory farms are unhealthy for animals.

- Eating meat is bad for the environment.

- The grain used to feed animals that are killed for food could be used instead to feed hungry people.

NO

- Animals can't think, so they don't have rights.

- Predators killing prey for food is part of nature.

- Not all meat comes from factory farms, and some animals raised for food live a good life before being eaten.

- Eating meat helped the human brain become more advanced.

- People need animal products such as meat to get vitamin B12 naturally.

This chart can help you form an educated, or informed, opinion about eating meat and understand why others might have a different point of view.

GLOSSARY

affect: To produce an effect on something.

Amazon rain forest: A large, warm, and wet forest in South America around the Amazon River.

debate: An argument or discussion about an issue, generally between two sides.

diet: The food and drink a person takes in.

encourage: To make someone more likely to do something.

environment: The natural world around us.

proof: Something that shows something else is true or correct.

publish: To print a written work and present it to the public.

ranch: A large farm for raising horses, cattle, or sheep.

vitamin: Something animals and plants need in small amounts to stay healthy.

For More
INFORMATION

WEBSITES

A Kid's Guide to Vegan Nutrition
www.petakids.com/food/kids-vegan-nutrition-guide/
PETA provides kids with a closer look at what vegans can eat to stay healthy, which is a good way to learn more about a vegan lifestyle.

"What's a Vegetarian?"
kidshealth.org/en/kids/vegetarian.html
This KidsHealth article offers readers facts about life as a vegetarian, including ways to make sure they get enough nutrients if they choose to stop eating meat.

BOOKS

Boothroyd, Jennifer. *Why Doesn't Everyone Eat Meat?: Vegetarianism and Special Diets.* Minneapolis, MN: Lerner Publishing Group, 2017.

Elton, Sarah, and Julie McLaughlin. *Meatless?: A Fresh Look at What You Eat.* Berkeley, CA: Owlkids Books, 2017.

Staniford, Linda. *How Do Animals Give Us Food?* Chicago, IL: Heinemann, 2017.

INDEX